This book belongs to

Th.   J.

THOMAS JEFFERSON

WRITTEN &
ILLUSTRATED BY
CHERYL HARNESS

NATIONAL GEOGRAPHIC
WASHINGTON, D.C.

"I have sworn upon the altar of God, eternal hostility against every form of tyranny over the mind of man."

THOMAS JEFFERSON, SEPTEMBER 23, 1800

A NOTE FROM THE AUTHOR

Thomas Jefferson had these words carved on his tombstone: "Author of the Declaration of Independence, of the Statute of Virginia for Religious Freedom, & Father of the University of Virginia." In truth, he could have added Scientist, Lawyer, Farmer, Architect, Diplomat, Inventor, Musician, Philosopher, and third President of the United States.

He was an extraordinary man living in a remarkable time. But he was also a man of contradictions. The brilliant scholar who wanted to "ride, serene and sublime above the concerns of this mortal world, contemplating truth and nature..." put himself at the center of a revolution, and then at the head of a government.

The contradiction that bothers people today the most has to do with slavery. On the one hand, Jefferson wrote "all Men are created equal." On the other he wrote that black people are inferior. He wrote and believed that God gave people the rights to "Life, Liberty, and the Pursuit of Happiness," but he never changed his own way of life, which depended on what he himself called an "abominable crime": the forced labor of his fellow human beings. Thomas said slavery was like having a "wolf by the ears, and we can neither hold him, nor safely let him go. Justice is in one scale, and self-preservation the other."

One part of his story is the story of Sally Hemings. She was the daughter of her mother's white master and half-sister of Jefferson's wife, Martha. When his father-in-law died, Thomas inherited 135 slaves, including Sally. Evidence now suggests that in the long years after Martha died, Sally Hemings and Thomas Jefferson, her owner, produced six children. Were Thomas and Sally in love, or was this a case of a master exploiting his slave? The wondering will never end.

What remains certain is that the United States of America, built upon the ideals of freedom and self-government, has lit up the world for more than two centuries. Whatever and whoever else he was, Thomas Jefferson helped to light the torch.

Peter and Jane Jefferson of Virginia had two little girls. On April 2, 1743, three-year old Jane and her two-year-old sister Mary got a red-headed baby brother named Thomas. After 1752, when a new calendar was adopted throughout the British Empire, Thomas Jefferson celebrated his birthday on April 13th. By then, Peter and Jane had three more daughters: Elizabeth, Martha, and Lucy. When Thomas was 12, his mother had twins: Anna and Randolph.

Peter Jefferson was an ambitious farmer and a surveyor—one who sets land boundaries—adventurous work in the wilderness. His neighbors elected him to their legislature, the House of Burgesses in Williamsburg. His slaves helped him farm his land and build his house, which he called Shadwell. He shared his love of horses and nature with his son Thomas. And his love of learning. Peter and Thomas wanted to know everything in and out of books.

The Jefferson children had a tutor, but when Thomas was nine, he began studying science, math, Latin, Greek, and French at a school for boys. In Thomas's time and place, most folks felt that serious book-learning was unnecessary for girls and downright unnatural for slaves.

The little schoolhouse was 50 miles away, too far to go home every day in that two-mile-an-hour horsepower world. For the next few years, Thomas stayed with the schoolmaster's family. He spent holidays and long, green summers at home. In the blue evenings, the Jeffersons sang and made music together. Thomas's big sister Jane played the harpsichord. With her encouragement, Thomas learned to play the violin.

The small circle of his family was broken when Thomas was 14 years old. Peter Jefferson died. Thomas, who'd grown tall, slender, and sturdy, like his dad, did what he would do again and again when his heart was full of sorrow. He put his head to work.

Peter had made certain that his son would get the education befitting what Thomas was: a bright young English aristocrat. Thomas began going to a small school led by the Reverend James Maury, a respected scholar. One of his other students, Dabney Carr, became Thomas's close friend. On weekends at Shadwell, they explored the wilderness by silent canoe or astride their horses. At parties, hunts, and country dances, they met their neighbors, such as fun-loving Patrick Henry, who was seven years their senior. Often folks danced their minuets and reels to the tune of Thomas's and Patrick's fiddles.

Thomas, his sisters, and Dabney often hiked to "Tom's Mountain," their favorite windy hilltop. Stretching out before them like the vast, misty valley below was a life of action and ideas. When Thomas was 16, he set off to find that life. He packed his saddlebags with his books and his fiddle. He was going to college.

When Thomas rode off, another young man rode along. His name was Jupiter. They were companions who trusted each other, but Jupiter would not be going to school. He was a slave: the permanent property of shy, idealistic Thomas Jefferson. Thomas would find knowledge at college, but neither he nor Jupiter would ever find the solution to the inequalities and contradictions of their world.

Thomas went to the College of William and Mary, named after a king and queen of England, in Williamsburg, the colonial capital of Virginia. He'd never seen such a big city before. More than 1,500 people! Not only did Thomas go to dances, plays, and horse races, he dove deeply into music, the "favorite passion" of his soul. He found time to spend with his friends, even though many a day he studied late into the night. Thomas was "bold in the pursuit of knowledge." His favorite teacher, a dignified Scotsman named Dr. William Small, introduced his brilliant student to those citizens of Williamsburg who shared Thomas's love of talk and music.

The WREN BUILDING at the COLLEGE of WILLIAM & MARY

Soon Thomas was playing his fiddle alongside the colonial governor, Francis Fauquier, and swimming in passionate talk with him, Professor Small, and a kind, intellectual lawyer, George Wythe. These earnest Englishmen talked about mathematics, law, geography, music, science, art, history, philosophy, and politics in the Colonies and across the sea, in the Parliament and court of their young king. As of 1760, they had a new ruler: His Majesty, George III.

Thomas finished with college in 1762 and began studying law. In his time, a young man who wanted to be a lawyer, as Thomas did, would "read law" and work with an established attorney such as Mr. Wythe. He became a fatherly mentor to Thomas, his intense, soft-spoken student. In his small, precise handwriting, Thomas kept careful notes about the law and anything else in the universe that interested him—poetry, mathematics, gardens, river navigation.

At Shadwell, he and his smart, much loved sister Jane talked about books and played music together. He rambled through the woods with Dabney, who had also become a lawyer. The two friends made a pact. In the far-off future, the one who died first would be buried by the other in their favorite place: on top of "Tom's Mountain."

It was during this time, in 1765, that lawmakers in the British Parliament—in which the American citizens of Great Britain had no say—decided that not only did the colonists have to provide lodging for the British soldiers in their midst, they had to buy royal tax stamps and stick them on playing cards and official documents. In Williamsburg, Thomas listened to his friend Patrick Henry, newly elected to the House of Burgesses, make a fiery speech against this "Stamp Act." What about their "sole right and power" as Englishmen to tax themselves? The question was a lightning bolt in a darkening sky.

Later in that fateful year, Thomas celebrated his little sister Martha's marriage to Dabney Carr, then was shocked with the sudden sickness and death of his sister, friend, and music partner: 25-year-old Jane.

Thomas fled to his work. He began practicing law in Virginia's various county courthouses. He heard lots of grumbling about lawmakers in London who'd undone the Stamp Act, but now there were taxes to be paid on goods imported from England such as glass, paper, and paint. After a lot of colonial uproar, those taxes were done away with in 1769—except for a small tax on tea. That shouldn't be a problem, the King's men figured. By then, Thomas's neighbors had elected him to the House of Burgesses. Now he could join the official debates, but like tall George Washington, Thomas preferred to listen.

The CAPITOL of the COLONY of VIRGINIA

When he wasn't worrying about the future of the Colonies, Thomas was studying drawings of Italian buildings and envisioning a house of his own on his hilltop back home. By the end of 1770, his slaves and hired workers had completed a one-room brick cottage. It was the beginning of a grand architecture experiment Thomas called Monticello, Italian for "little mountain." It was to this cottage, through a black night deep with snow, that Thomas would bring his bride.

He met her in Williamsburg. She was a pretty, copper-haired widow who shared his love of books and music. Thomas and 23-year-old Martha—he called her "Patty"—Skelton married each other on the first day of 1772. From the little brick cottage came the sounds of Martha's harpsichord, Thomas's violin, and, in the fall, the cries of a baby daughter.

At the edges of their happiness, trouble clouds loomed. In the spring of 1773, not long before Martha's father died, Dabney Carr died of typhoid fever. In December 1773, far to the north of Dabney's grave on Monticello, where boys had imagined their future, men were dropping boxes of British tea into icy Boston Harbor.

Trouble! If His furious Majesty King George III could shut down Massachusetts's main harbor and send red-coated troops—which he did—then all 13 Colonies faced trouble. Worried Virginians fasted and prayed for divine guidance. Thomas carefully reasoned out and wrote "A Summary View of the Rights of British America." It was printed in pamphlets and added to the letters that were beginning to circulate in saddlebags up and down the Colonies. Patriots admired Thomas's writing and agreed with him that "the legislature of one part of the empire" had no business trampling on the God-given rights of another.

The colonists began choosing delegates to meet in a "Continental Congress" in Philadelphia, Pennsylvania, in September 1774. There they'd plan how to get their king to treat his American subjects respectfully, as free British citizens—something that most colonists were very proud to be.

Americans, the Congress decided, would stop trading with Britain. They'd drink coffee or cider—anything rather than taxed tea—and wear American homespun clothing. Some were cautiously storing up weapons and ammunition in case of trouble.

Trouble! Past-the-point-of-no-return kind of trouble broke out between British soldiers and Massachusetts patriots on April 19, 1775. Soon, 32-year-old Thomas was making the hard 250-mile journey to Philadelphia to the second Continental Congress. After a year of debate and turmoil, the time had come for Americans to demand, as Patrick Henry once said, "liberty or death."

Because delegates such as John Adams, a Boston lawyer, and Benjamin Franklin, the famous Philadelphia inventor and scientist, knew Thomas to be a fine writer and a scholar, they asked him to tell the world what many colonists believed and why they were committing revolution. It took Thomas two hot weeks to compose America's shocking manifesto. Most people believed it was God who put monarchs on their powerful thrones. Americans were doing something entirely

PENNSYLVANIA STATE HOUSE

now Known as INDEPENDENCE HALL

THE SECOND CONTINENTAL CONGRESS

new and possibly sinful: quitting the British Empire without the King's permission! They meant to make a nation based on the ideas that all men were born free, "created equal," with leaders whose power came from the "Consent of the Governed."

The delegates debated and changed some of the wording—much to Thomas's dismay. Then, on July 2, 1776, they agreed to break away from Britain. Two days later, on the 4th, once they pledged to each other "our Lives, our Fortunes, and our sacred Honor," they knew they'd be traitors to their King. They'd face the wrath of the most powerful empire on Earth. They might be signing their death warrants the minute they signed the Declaration of Independence.

In New York that summer, patriotism was turning to panic. General George Washington was leading his inexperienced Continental Army in a hopeless battle to defend Manhattan from the King's "redcoats." Thomas hurried home to his wife, still sick and sad over the death of their baby, Jane. Another baby girl and boy would die before the awful war ended. With each loss, Martha's health faded.

In Virginia, Thomas worked on state laws that would shape the nation-to-be, especially that of the separation of government from the free practice of one's religion. He began recording his scientific and philosophical observations—including thoughts about his and his country's addiction to the "abominable crime" of slavery—in his one book, *Notes on the State of Virginia (1781–1785):* "...I tremble for my country when I reflect that God is just: that justice cannot sleep forever."

After Virginians elected Thomas to be their governor in 1779, their capital was moved inland to Richmond, away, they hoped, from attack by sea. Not far enough! Thomas narrowly escaped capture when royal warships came sailing up the James River. By October 1781, Thomas had refused a third term as governor, and America had, with the help of France, won a final victory at Yorktown, Virginia. Less than a year later, Thomas's "dear companion" Martha died after she had their sixth baby. The father of three little girls was lost in grief. For months, there was no escape.

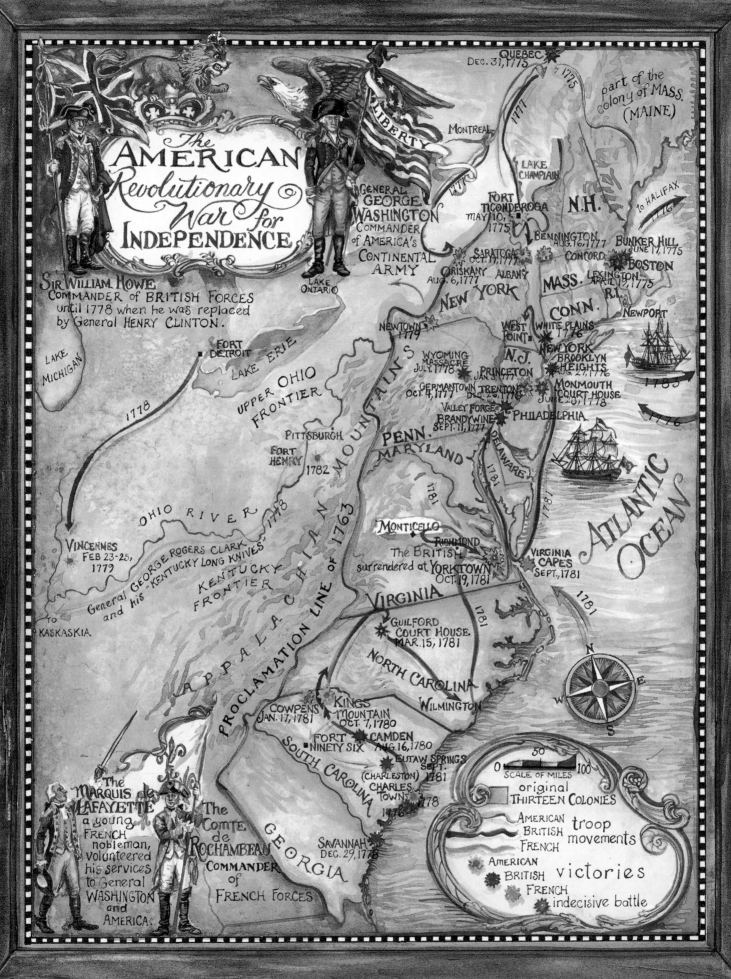

The
AMERICAN
Revolutionary
War for
INDEPENDENCE

LIBERTY

General
GEORGE
WASHINGTON
COMMANDER
of AMERICA'S
CONTINENTAL
ARMY

Sir WILLIAM HOWE
COMMANDER of BRITISH FORCES
until 1778 when he was replaced
by General HENRY CLINTON.

QUEBEC
DEC. 31, 1775

MONTREAL

1775
1777

part of the
colony of MASS.
(MAINE)

to HALIFAX
1776

LAKE
CHAMPLAIN

FORT
TICONDEROGA
MAY 10,
1775

N.H.

BENNINGTON
AUG.16,1777

BUNKER HILL
JUNE 17, 1775

SARATOGA
OCT.17,1777

CONCORD

BOSTON

ORISKANY
AUG. 6, 1777

ALBANY

MASS.

LEXINGTON
APRIL 19, 1775

NEW YORK

R.I.

CONN.

LAKE
ONTARIO

NEWTOWN
1779

WYOMING
MASSACRE
JULY 1778

WEST
POINT

WHITE
PLAINS
1776

NEWPORT

LAKE
MICHIGAN

FORT
DETROIT

LAKE ERIE

UPPER OHIO
FRONTIER

1778

GERMANTOWN
OCT.4,1777

N.J.

PRINCETON
JAN.3,1777

NEW YORK
BROOKLYN
HEIGHTS
AUG. 27, 1776

TRENTON
DEC.26,1776

MONMOUTH
COURT HOUSE
JUNE 28, 1778

1783

PITTSBURGH

FORT
HENRY
1782

PENN.

MARYLAND

VALLEY FORGE
BRANDYWINE
SEPT. 11, 1777

PHILADELPHIA

DELAWARE

1781

1776

OHIO RIVER

1778

VINCENNES
FEB 23-25,
1779

General GEORGE ROGERS CLARK
and his "Kentucky Long Knives"
1778

KENTUCKY
FRONTIER

to
KASKASKIA

APPALACHIAN MOUNTAINS

PROCLAMATION LINE of 1763

MONTICELLO

RICHMOND

The BRITISH
surrendered at YORKTOWN
OCT. 19, 1781

VIRGINIA
CAPES
SEPT., 1781

ATLANTIC
OCEAN

VIRGINIA

GUILFORD
COURT HOUSE
MAR. 15, 1781

1781

1781

NORTH CAROLINA

WILMINGTON

N
E
S
W

COWPENS
JAN. 17, 1781

KINGS
MOUNTAIN
OCT. 7, 1780

FORT
NINETY SIX

CAMDEN
AUG.16,1780

EUTAW SPRINGS
SEPT.
1781

SOUTH CAROLINA

(CHARLESTON)
CHARLES
TOWN
1778
1776

0   50   100
SCALE OF MILES

original
THIRTEEN COLONIES

AMERICAN
BRITISH
FRENCH
troop
movements

AMERICAN
BRITISH victories
FRENCH
indecisive battle

The
MARQUIS de
LAFAYETTE
a young
FRENCH
nobleman,
volunteered
his services
to General
WASHINGTON
and
AMERICA.

The
COMTE
de
ROCHAMBEAU
COMMANDER
of
FRENCH FORCES

GEORGIA

SAVANNAH
DEC. 29, 1778

He turned again to work. In 1783, he was elected to the United States Congress, meeting in Annapolis, Maryland. One of his tasks there was planning the republic's money, based on a ten-dimed dollar. In the spring of 1784, the Congress sent Thomas on a mission. Thomas left his two younger girls with their mother's sister, then he, his 12-year-old Martha (her dad called her "Patsy"), and a slave, James Hemings, set off for France. Thomas joined his old friends Ben Franklin and John and Abigail Adams trying to win European trade and loans for their weak, young nation.

Sorrow followed him across the ocean.

This ancient Roman temple at NÎMES, FRANCE was TOM'S inspiration for this design of VIRGINIA'S capitol at Richmond 1785

KING LOUIS XVI QUEEN MARIE ANTOINETTE

When he heard that his baby, 3-year-old Lucy, had gotten sick and died, wretched Thomas sent for his daughter Mary ("Polly") so he could have what was left of his family all together. A 14-year-old slave, Sally Hemings, accompanied 8-year-old Polly to Paris.

In Europe, Thomas studied everything that could improve America: trees, crops, vineyards, and buildings. He loved the brilliant culture of France, but not her monarchs, who ignored their hungry people and wide-eyed talk of Liberté—like in America! In England, he gloried in the gardens, but King George III wasn't at all prepared to be polite to the author of the Declaration of Independence.

We the People of the United States, in Order to Form a more perfect Union, establish Justice, insure domestic Tranquility, provide for the common defense, promote the general Welfare, and secure the Blessings of Liberty to ourselves and our Posterity do ordain and establish this Constitution for the United States of America.

Sailing ships carried letters between Thomas and his friend James Madison about the growing turmoil in Paris and the discussions going on in Philadelphia in 1787. Fifty-five men including Madison and George Washington were working out a firm government for the United States. The sturdy, elastic U.S. Constitution went into effect in 1789, and on the 30th of April, George Washington became the nation's first President.

Ten weeks later, after Washington's Inauguration, France exploded into revolution. Thomas believed that "a little rebellion now and then was a good thing," but, still, he was anxious to get his family away from danger. They set sail in the fall for Virginia.

Soon Thomas had to choose between joy at being home at Monticello and his patriotic duty to his nation and President Washington. He made the hard choice. Soon, as Secretary of State,

Jefferson was caught up in a powerful argument about the workings of the government. This naturally led to Americans choosing sides.

George Washington and his Vice President, John Adams, disliked the idea of political parties, but they tended to agree with Secretary of the Treasury Alexander Hamilton, who thought that a strong central, or "federal," government was good for business. These so-called Federalists tended to disagree with "Democratic-Republicans" such as Thomas Jefferson and James Madison, who generally wanted stronger rights for states and individuals and less for the central government at Philadelphia.

In 1790, the Congress decided that—no later than 1800—the capital should be more centrally located, in a "District of Columbia" between Maryland and Virginia. Thomas, who was full of ideas from the buildings he'd seen in Europe, worked closely with the architects of the new "federal city." The modest President didn't call it "Washington."

*Tom secretly entered the design contest. He signed his drawing "A.Z."

After the President's first term, Thomas resigned his job in 1793. He was homesick and done with politics—he thought.

When tired-out George Washington refused a third term, the Democratic-Republicans nominated a very reluctant Thomas to run against Federalist John Adams. The law changed later on, but in 1796, the runner-up in the election automatically became the winner's Vice President—even if they were in opposing political parties. This is what happened when John Adams narrowly won the race. Dutiful Thomas found himself in a bouncing coach on the deep-rutted trail from Monticello to Philadelphia.

The debate about how the government should work went on—in fact, it still does. It didn't help that France and England, old enemies, wanted to stop anyone from trading with the other. French warships were attacking U.S. merchant ships. Many Federalists called for war on France even if she had helped America win independence. Vice President Jefferson and his party thought the U.S. should stick by France and the ideals of the French Revolution even if it had resulted in thousands of executions.

America was like a mouse batted around by French and English cats. John Adams wanted the mouse to be neutral—and uneaten! But talk grew so hot that his Federalist Party in Congress passed laws against criticizing the government. Foreign critics could be thrown in jail or out of the country. Dark days for civil rights, Thomas thought. He saw the election of 1800 as being "as real a revolution in the principles of our government as that of 1776." He was no reluctant candidate this time. The race between the Democratic-Republicans and the Federalists was tough and mean. It resulted in hard, hurt feelings between Jefferson and Adams, the old revolutionary comrades. A stagecoach carrying the second President rattled out of town hours before Thomas left his boarding house on the morning of March 4, 1801. He walked to the partly finished Capitol, and there he became the third President of the United States, the first to be inaugurated in the city of Washington.

Visitors to the unfinished President's House were surprised by Thomas's worn slippers and by his manners, which were less formal than those of his two predecessors. Thomas thought that the leader of a republic should live simply. Visitors to his office—in the present-day State Dining Room—would see evidence of Thomas's curious mind: maps, charts, globes, a telescope, a thermometer, a "polygraph" (which allowed Thomas to make copies of his letters), plants in clay pots and bell jars, his violin, and a cage where his pet mockingbird lived—

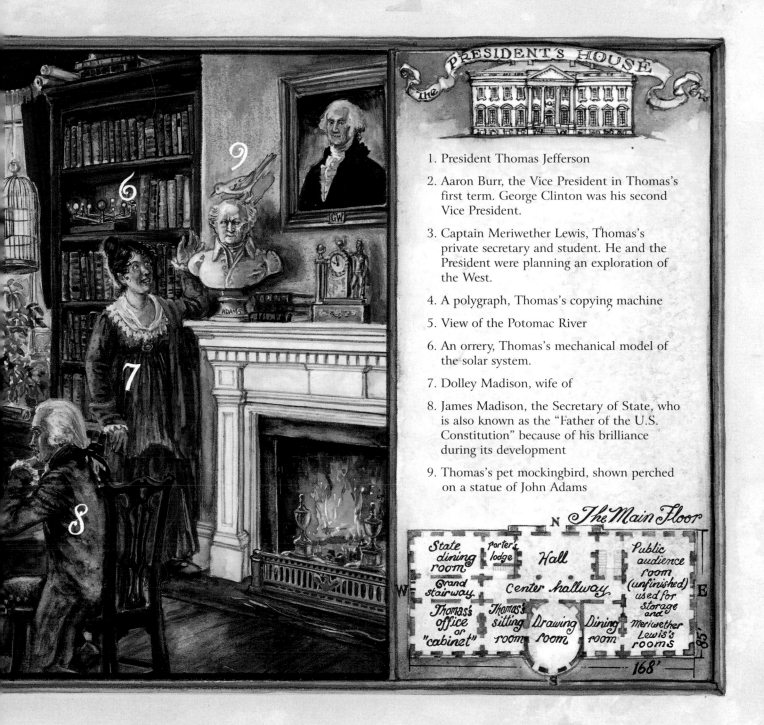

THE PRESIDENT'S HOUSE

1. President Thomas Jefferson

2. Aaron Burr, the Vice President in Thomas's first term. George Clinton was his second Vice President.

3. Captain Meriwether Lewis, Thomas's private secretary and student. He and the President were planning an exploration of the West.

4. A polygraph, Thomas's copying machine

5. View of the Potomac River

6. An orrery, Thomas's mechanical model of the solar system.

7. Dolley Madison, wife of

8. James Madison, the Secretary of State, who is also known as the "Father of the U.S. Constitution" because of his brilliance during its development

9. Thomas's pet mockingbird, shown perched on a statue of John Adams

The Main Floor

State dining room | Porter's lodge | Hall | Public audience room (unfinished) used for storage and Meriwether Lewis's rooms

Grand stairway | Center hallway

Thomas's office or "cabinet" | Thomas's sitting room | Drawing room | Dining room

168'

85'

when it wasn't flying about the room or sitting on Thomas's shoulder. The visitors Thomas was most eager to see were his daughters and their families. He was often lonely in the big stone President's House, which seemed to him "big enough for two emperors, one Pope, and the Grand Lama."

Sometimes, Dolley Madison, the wife of James, his Secretary of State, helped Thomas greet his guests, who delighted in his macaroni, ice cream, and other European delicacies.

LAND CLAIMED BY U.S. AND BRITAIN

FORT MANDAN
winter camp near a village of friendly MANDAN Indians
Nov. 2, 1804 ~ APRIL 6, 1805

MARIAS RIVER

JULY 27, 1806 A deadly fight with BLACKFEET warriors

LEWIS MISSOURI RIVER

JULY 3, 1806 The expedition splits up.

LEWIS

GREAT FALLS OF THE MISSOURI

YELLOWSTONE RIVER

AUG. 12, 1806 Homebound adventurers reunite.

THREE FORKS CLARK

CLARK

FORT CLATSOP COLUMBIA RIVER
Cold, rainy, hungry winter camp
DEC. 8, 1805 ~ MARCH 23, 1806

NEZ PERCE villages

LOLO trail in the treacherous BITTERROOT MOUNTAINS

OREGON COUNTRY
desired by RUSSIA, BRITAIN, and the U.S.

SHOSHONE villages

SNAKE RIVER

AUG. 17, 1805 CAMP FORTUNATE
SACAGAWEA is reunited with her brother, a SHOSHONE chief.

YORK, EXPLORER and CLARK'S SLAVE.

CLARK

LEWIS

SEPT. 7, 1804 A discovery: prairie dogs!

PLATTE RIVER

"Ocian in view! O! the joy."
William CLARK
Nov. 7, 1805

SPANISH EMPIRE

CAPTAINS

GREAT SALT LAKE

NOV. 4, 1804
The captains meet a FRENCH-CANADIAN trapper who had won his teenage SHOSHONE wife on a bet from the HIDATSA raiders who had kidnapped her.
Not only did SACAGAWEA endure the explorers' terrible journey over the mountains to the sea and back, She helped to guide the CORPS of DISCOVERY as well as translate for them. All the while, she cared for her baby boy, JEAN BAPTISTE CHARBONNEAU, born FEB. 11, 1805.

SEAMAN, LEWIS's Newfoundland dog

Toussaint CHARBONNEAU

SACAGAWEA "BIRD WOMAN"

LOUISIANA PURCHASE
LOUISIANA TERRITORY as of 1805

The most important thing that happened to his nation in Thomas's presidency was the purchase of almost a million square miles of deep forest and tall grass west of the Mississippi River. As the native peoples, beasts, and birds who lived there may not have known, rulers of faraway France and Spain claimed ownership of this land of "Louisiana" at one time or another. In 1803, France's new young leader, Napoleon Bonaparte, needed money to go to war with England. He offered the Louisiana Territory to the United States—for $15 million, a bargain!

Thomas had dreamed of exploration into the mysterious West. What animals, plants, and civilizations were out there? Could there be a waterway through the northwest to speed trade with lands beyond the Pacific Ocean? (No.) He pushed the Louisiana Purchase Treaty through the Congress. On December 20, 1803, the U.S. took possession of the lands. Five months later, Thomas's trusted 29-year-old secretary, whose name was Meriwether Lewis, 33-year-old Captain William Clark, and about 40 others set out from where the Missouri River flows into the Mississippi. They were off to explore what Thomas called an "empire of liberty" beyond the setting sun.

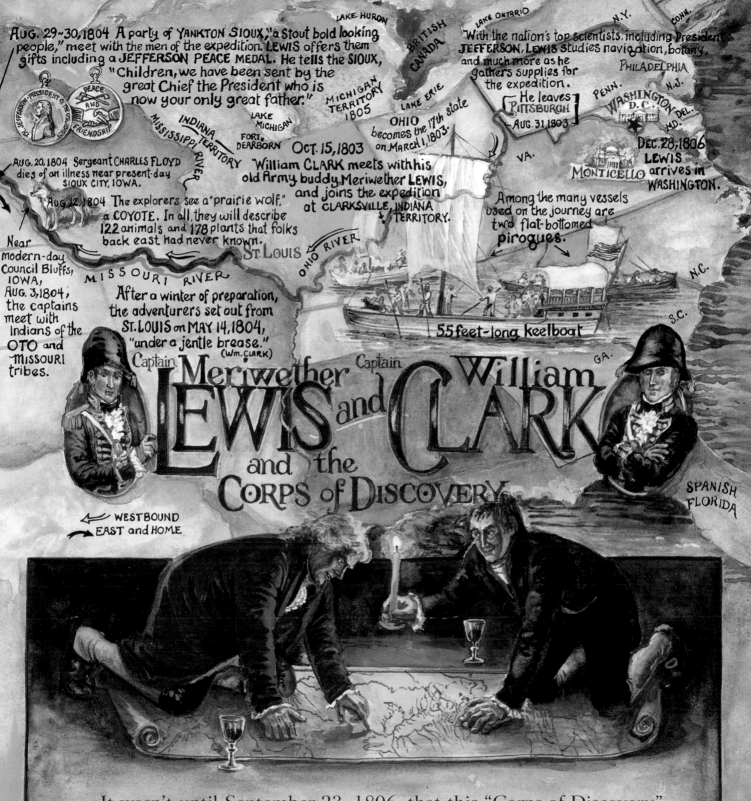

AUG. 29~30,1804 A party of YANKTON SIOUX, "a Stout bold looking people," meet with the men of the expedition. LEWIS offers them gifts including a JEFFERSON PEACE MEDAL. He tells the SIOUX, "Children, we have been sent by the great Chief the President who is now your only great father."

With the nation's top scientists, including President JEFFERSON, LEWIS studies navigation, botany, and much more as he gathers supplies for the expedition.
He leaves PITTSBURGH AUG. 31,1803.

AUG. 20,1804 Sergeant CHARLES FLOYD dies of an illness near present-day SIOUX CITY, IOWA.

AUG. 12,1804 The explorers see a "prairie wolf," a COYOTE. In all, they will describe 122 animals and 178 plants that folks back east had never known.

OHIO becomes the 17th state on MARCH 1,1803.

OCT. 15,1803 William CLARK meets with his old Army buddy, Meriwether LEWIS, and joins the expedition at CLARKSVILLE, INDIANA TERRITORY.

DEC.28,1806 LEWIS arrives in WASHINGTON.

MONTICELLO

Near modern-day Council Bluffs, IOWA, AUG. 3,1804, the captains meet with Indians of the OTO and MISSOURI tribes.

After a winter of preparation, the adventurers set out from ST. LOUIS on MAY 14,1804, "under a jentle brease." (WM. CLARK)

Among the many vessels used on the journey are two flat-bottomed pirogues.

55 feet-long keelboat

Captain Meriwether LEWIS and Captain William CLARK and the CORPS of DISCOVERY

⟵ WESTBOUND
⟵ EAST and HOME

LAKE HURON
LAKE ONTARIO
N.Y.
CONN.
BRITISH CANADA
PHILADELPHIA
PENN.
N.J.
WASHINGTON D.C.
DEL.
MD.
MICHIGAN TERRITORY 1805
LAKE ERIE
VA.
INDIANA TERRITORY
LAKE MICHIGAN
FORT DEARBORN
MISSISSIPPI RIVER
ST. LOUIS
OHIO RIVER
MISSOURI RIVER
N.C.
S.C.
GA.
SPANISH FLORIDA

It wasn't until September 23, 1806, that this "Corps of Discovery" made it back to St. Louis—with what stories to tell! At the end of that year, Lewis unrolled the map, drawn by Clark, and spread it on the floor in the President's House. The young explorer and the 63-year-old President got down on their hands and knees to trace the rivers with their fingers.

Thomas saw the presidency as a "splendid misery." When his second term ended in 1809 and James Madison took office, Thomas said, "never did a prisoner, released from his chains, feel such a relief." Every Monticello morning, as soon as he had enough light to see the clock at the foot of his bed, Thomas got up to pursue all sorts of happiness: music, carpentry, botany, and astronomy. He kept meticulous records of the weather, his farms, and experiments with crop rotation and new plant species. "Ardent farmer" Thomas even developed a more efficient plow.

"Monticello

Thomas Jefferson's "essay in architecture"

At first, Thomas wanted the house to look like this.

The house and his ideas expanded over the years between 1768 and 1826.

James and Dolley Madison slept in the North Octagonal Room when they came to visit.

NORTH TERRACE
NORTH PIAZZA
TEA ROOM
DINING ROOM
ALCOVE BED
BED
NORTH SQUARE ROOM
WEST PORTICO
PARLOR
BALCONY
ENTRANCE HALL
EAST PORTICO (front porch)
Thomas's BEDROOM
BED
CABINET
window shutters
In the FAMILY SITTING ROOM Thomas's grandchildren studied their lessons.
BOOK ROOM
SOUTH PIAZZA (GREENHOUSE)
SOUTH TERRACE

There are eleven rooms on the FIRST FLOOR.

There are six more rooms upstairs and four more on the THIRD FLOOR.

Thomas's bed was in an alcove between his bedroom and his study that Thomas called his CABINET.

The ENTRANCE HALL

Cannonball weights powered the SEVEN DAY CALENDAR CLOCK.

Sunday
Monday
Tuesday
Wednesday
Thursday
Friday

Saturday's marker is in the CELLAR.

He called Monticello his "essay in architecture." Thomas's remote, beautiful, never-quite-finished hilltop house seemed to sum up the ingenious man who lived there, from the maps and calendar clock in the front hall to the mechanical dumbwaiters in the dining room to the plaster busts of those he admired: George Washington, fellow scientist Benjamin Franklin, and the Marquis de Lafayette, the French aristocrat who had fought for American independence.

Thomas had a dumbwaiter which could bring wine up from the cellar to the DINING Room.

The KITCHEN was below the SOUTH TERRACE

Marquis de Lafayette

John Paul Jones

Benjamin Franklin

TEA ROOM

George Washington

The PARLOR

And books. A world of knowledge was in his personal library of more than 6,000 books. During the War of 1812, Thomas heard that British troops not only had torched the President's House, but also had burned the Capitol and, with it, the government's library. Thomas, who believed that only an educated people could fully take part in democracy, offered his beloved collection for sale to the nation—for the people. He got $25,000. The people got the beginning of the Library of Congress.

Then Thomas bought more books. He couldn't live without them.

Monticello

THE GROVE, a tree garden which Thomas designed in 1806.

1. NORTH PAVILION

CISTERN

2. NORTH TERRACE underground PASSAGEWAY

Rainwater collected in CISTERN

4. SOUTH TERRACE

6. STONE HOUSE for FREE WORKMEN

SLAVE DWELLING

WEST FRONT

3. SOUTH PAVILION

LABYRINTH

WEST LAWN

Thomas laid out the WINDING WALK and flower beds and borders in 1808.

Thomas's land, nearly 5,000 acres, was divided into four farms: SHADWELL, LEGO, TUFTON, and of course, MONTICELLO, "home farm."

Free EUROPEANS, AMERICANS, and enslaved AFRICAN AMERICANS lived and worked on MULBERRY ROW.

ORNAMENTAL FISH POND

WASH HOUSE

SMOKEHOUSE - DAIRY

5.

STORE HOUSE

PRIVY

FIRST of FOUR "ROUNDABOUTS"

BLACKSMITH'S SHOP and NAILERY

to the GRAVEYARD

SAWPIT

3. JOINERY

2. VEGETABLE

CARPENTER'S SHOP

STONE WALL

CHARCOAL SHED

About a dozen free craftsmen and overseers and 130 enslaved men, women, and children helped turn Thomas's dream of Monticello into reality. They worked sunrise to sundown, six days a week, in the kitchen, stables, gardens, dairy, workshops, vineyards, orchards, and fields. Enslaved servants offered hospitality to the many visitors, such as James and Dolley Madison, whose carriages rattled up the rough road to Thomas's hilltop home.

Tourists came, hoping to get a glimpse of Thomas. They tramped in his yard and stood in his front hall to ponder the display of Indian artifacts and nature specimens brought by Lewis and Clark from the West.

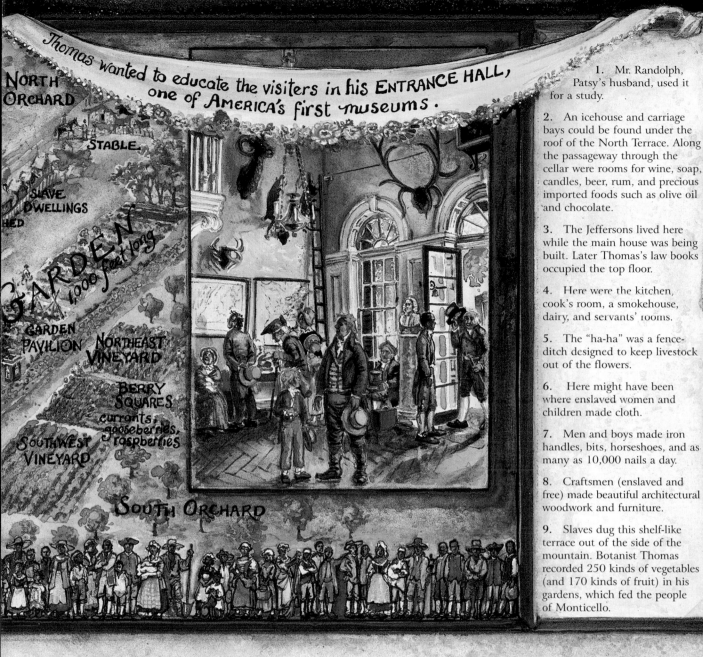

Thomas wanted to educate the visiters in his ENTRANCE HALL, one of AMERICA's first museums.

NORTH ORCHARD

STABLE

SLAVE DWELLINGS

SHED

GARDEN 1000 feet long

GARDEN PAVILION

NORTHEAST VINEYARD

BERRY SQUARES currants, gooseberries, raspberries

SOUTHWEST VINEYARD

SOUTH ORCHARD

1. Mr. Randolph, Patsy's husband, used it for a study.

2. An icehouse and carriage bays could be found under the roof of the North Terrace. Along the passageway through the cellar were rooms for wine, soap, candles, beer, rum, and precious imported foods such as olive oil and chocolate.

3. The Jeffersons lived here while the main house was being built. Later Thomas's law books occupied the top floor.

4. Here were the kitchen, cook's room, a smokehouse, dairy, and servants' rooms.

5. The "ha-ha" was a fence-ditch designed to keep livestock out of the flowers.

6. Here might have been where enslaved women and children made cloth.

7. Men and boys made iron handles, bits, horseshoes, and as many as 10,000 nails a day.

8. Craftsmen (enslaved and free) made beautiful architectural woodwork and furniture.

9. Slaves dug this shelf-like terrace out of the side of the mountain. Botanist Thomas recorded 250 kinds of vegetables (and 170 kinds of fruit) in his gardens, which fed the people of Monticello.

They talked with the many children who lived at Monticello. Thomas's sister, Martha, who was Dabney Carr's widow, lived there with her family. So did his daughter Patsy, her husband, and their 11 children. Thomas loved having his young relatives close by.

The country's farm economy was poor in these times, and life at Monticello was costly. Although the money from the sale of his books helped, Thomas was so tormented with debt that he and his extended family nearly lost their hilltop home. Only donations from grateful citizens of the nation he'd helped to create allowed Thomas to spend his last years in Monticello.

MONTICELLO

In 1812, John Adams made the first move toward patching up an old friendship. He sent a letter to Monticello. Thomas wrote back to the round-faced man he'd met in 1775, back when they were "fellow laborers in the same cause, struggling for what is most valuable to man: his right of self-government." They carried on a deep and lively conversation of many letters. And on a fall evening in 1824, Thomas waited on his front porch to greet another old patriot. The old Virginian and an old Frenchman, the Marquis de Lafayette, wept as they embraced.

In his last years, Thomas poured his thoughts and energy into the creation of a public college based upon the unlimited "freedom of the human mind." In the spring of 1825, forty scholars came to study the books he had chosen, in the ten pavilions of learning he had designed. Snowy-haired Thomas took the deepest satisfaction in the opening of the University of Virginia.

Thomas designed this ROTUNDA for the University of VIRGINIA

By the time spring came again, 83-year-old Thomas Jefferson and his old "fellow laborer," 90-year-old John Adams, were both weak and sick, but they willed themselves to stay alive. There was a special anniversary coming.

Not long before John Adams died in the early evening of the Glorious Fourth of July, 1826, he whispered, "Thomas Jefferson still survives." It wasn't the truth. Thomas, surrounded by his family, had died shortly before one o'clock that afternoon, 50 years after the first Independence Day.

Thomas was buried beside Martha, the sweetheart of his youth, near their dead children, near his boyhood friend, on top of his mountain. His portion of the earth belongs, as Thomas once wrote, "to the living, not to the dead." When the living come to pay their respects to the Sage of Monticello, Thomas may or may not be there. His spirit and the souls of those who shared his windy mountaintop are free.

The WORLD of PRESIDENT

In Thomas's two terms as President, 1801–1809, in the first decade of the 19th century, the young republic stood up to pirates, tried to face down France and Great Britain, acquired a 17th state, and nearly doubled its size. His Vice President took part in a murderous duel, then a mysterious plot. A painful accusation then a dreadful loss came to the President himself.

THOMAS JEFFERSON

★ June 10, 1801 The Barbary State of Tripoli declared war on America. Since the 1500s, any country's merchant ships sailing on the Mediterranean Sea could be attacked by Barbary pirates. They demanded fortunes in "tribute." Now they demanded more. The tiny U.S. Navy sailed into action, then earned for America a peace treaty in June 1805 and a bit of respect.

★ July 4, 1802 The U.S. Military Academy at West Point, New York, opened.

★ September 1, 1802 Journalist James Callender published an accusation in a Federalist newspaper: President Jefferson fathered children by his slave Sally Hemings, the so-called "African Venus." Thomas refused to comment on what he called "federal slander." (The dead take their secrets with them.)

★ January 18, 1803 Thomas asked the Congress for $2,500 to pay for a "Voyage of Discovery" to the Pacific Ocean.

★ March 1, 1803 Ohio became the 17th state.

★ May 2, 1803 Papers (dated April 30) were signed in which the U.S. Government agreed to pay Napoleon Bonaparte, the leader of France, $15 million for 827,987 square miles of Louisiana Purchase land.

★ May 16, 1803 England declared war on France. Thomas, wanting to keep out of it, tried but failed to stop trade with both nations.

★ 1804 German geographer Alexander von Humboldt ended his five-year exploration of Mexico and Central and South America.

★ April 17, 1804 Thomas's 26-year-old daughter Mary (aka Polly or Maria) died not long after having her second child.

★ May 14, 1804 William Clark, Meriwether Lewis, and the Corps of Discovery set out from St. Louis, Missouri, on their expedition. They returned on September 23, 1806.

★ July 11, 1804 Thomas's Vice President, Aaron Burr, challenged, shot, and killed former Secretary of the Treasury Alexander Hamilton in a duel. Later, Burr was charged with trying to win his own empire in the West.

★ December 2, 1804 Napoleon Bonaparte, a Corsican soldier who had risen out of the blood and ashes of the French Revolution, crowned himself Emperor of France.

★ February 11, 1805 Sacagawea, a guide and translator for the Corps of Discovery, gave birth to a baby boy at Fort Mandan, near present-day Bismark, North Dakota.

★ April 2, 1805 Author Hans Christian Andersen was born in Denmark.

★ January 17, 1806 Martha (aka Patsy) Thomas's only living child, gave birth to James Madison Randolph, the first child to be born in the White House.

★ March 2, 1807 Congress passed a law: As of January 1, 1808, it would be against the law to import slaves from Africa.

★ August 17, 1807 Robert Fulton's steamboat *Clermont* sailed up the Hudson River.

★ 1808 Ludwig von Beethoven wrote Symphonies No. 5 and No. 6. John Chapman (aka Johnny Appleseed) was planting frontier orchards.

★ September 8, 1808 The Osage Indians signed over their lands (most of present-day Missouri and northern Arkansas) to the U.S. government. The Osage moved to present-day Oklahoma.

★ February 12, 1809 Abraham Lincoln was born in Kentucky and naturalist Charles Darwin was born in England.

★ March 4, 1809 James Madison became the fourth President.

★ October 11, 1809 Meriwether Lewis died in Tennessee.

To S.P.F., V.G., and K.B.

BIBLIOGRAPHY

Adams, William Howard. *Jefferson's Monticello.* New York: Abbeville Press, 1983

Adams, William Howard. *The Paris Years of Thomas Jefferson.* New Haven, Conn.: Yale University Press, 1997

Bober, Natalie S. *Thomas Jefferson, Man on a Mountain.* New York: Simon and Schuster, 1988

Fleming, Thomas. *Liberty, The American Revolution.* New York: Viking, 1997

Jones, Veda Boyd. *Thomas Jefferson.* Philadelphia: Chelsea House, 2000

Nardo, Don. *The Importance of Thomas Jefferson.* San Diego: Lucent Books, 1993

Seale, William. *The President's House.* Washington, D.C.: White House Historical Association, 1986

ACKNOWLEDGMENTS

I wish to thank designer David M. Seager and those who tend Thomas's great work of art and totally recommend a visit to Monticello in Charlottesville, Virginia.

NOTES ON THE QUOTATIONS

Quotes from Thomas Jefferson were taken from *The Writings of Thomas Jefferson,* edited by A.A. Lipscomb and A.E. Bergh. Washington, D.C.: Thomas Jefferson Memorial Association, 1903

The pictures of Mrs. Jefferson (pages 19 & 24), of whom no portrait survives, are products of the illustrator's imagination.

You can find excellent information about Thomas and his world at www.monticello.org. Teachers who wish to schedule study tours for their students may write to this address: Monticello Education Department, P.O. Box 316, Charlottesville, Virginia 22902 (434) 984-9853

Cheryl Harness does her illustrations on Strathmore cold-pressed illustration board, using watercolor, gouache, ink, and colored pencil.

Text is set in Arrus BT, by Bitstream Inc.

Library of Congress Cataloging-in-Publication Data
Harness, Cheryl.
Thomas Jefferson / written and illustrated by Cheryl Harness.
p. cm.
Summary: Examines the life and times of the multifaceted man who wrote the Declaration of Independence and later became the third president of the United States.
ISBN 0-7922-6496-7
1. Jefferson, Thomas, 1743–1826—Juvenile literature. 2.
Presidents—United States—Biography—Juvenile literature.
[1. Jefferson, Thomas, 1743–1826. 2. Presidents.] I. Title.
E332.79.H38 2004
973.4'6'092--dc21

2003005853

One of the world's largest nonprofit scientific and educational organizations, the National Geographic Society was founded in 1888 "for the increase and diffusion of geographic knowledge." Fulfilling this mission, the Society educates and inspires millions every day through its magazines, books, television programs, videos, maps and atlases, research grants, the National Geographic Bee, teacher workshops, and innovative classroom materials. The Society is supported through membership dues, charitable gifts, and income from the sale of its educational products. This support is vital to National Geographic's mission to increase global understanding and promote conservation of our planet through exploration, research, and education.

For more information, please call 1-800-NGS LINE (647-5463) or write to the following address:

NATIONAL GEOGRAPHIC SOCIETY
1145 17th Street N.W.
Washington, D.C. 20036-4688 U.S.A.
Visit the Society's Web site: www.nationalgeographic.com

Printed in Belgium